THE TOTALLY
AWESOME
WORLD OF

CRISTIANO
RONALDO

LEARN ALL THERE IS TO KNOW ABOUT YOUR FAVORITE SOCCER LEGEND

—

NEAL E. FISCHER

becker&mayer! kids

CONTENTS

INTRODUCTION

I t was a Sunday in Paris in July 2016, the air thick with anticipation for the Euro final. Nearly 80,000 fans packed into the Stade de France in hopes of watching their hometown team win a third championship. Standing in their way was the Portuguese national team led by their captain, Cristiano Ronaldo, the world's greatest striker. But to Cristiano and his teammates, this was more than just a game and more than just a trophy—it was a chance at redemption.

Twelve years earlier, Portugal had hosted the 2004 Euro tournament and, like France, made it to the final match. In front of his own country, the then–17-year-old Cristiano saw his dreams shatter when Portugal lost the final to Greece in a heartbreaking defeat. The game left Cristiano in tears.

What Are the EUROS?

The UEFA Euro Championship (often called the Euros) is a major international soccer tournament that started in 1960 and is held every four years, like the Olympics. Instead of a global invitation to compete, the Euros focus on national teams from across Europe. It's the second-most-watched football tournament in the world after the FIFA World Cup. In 2024, 53 nations entered the tournament and were whittled down to twenty-four finalists competing for the Henri Delaunay Trophy. Spain ultimately proved victorious by defeating England 2-1 to win their fourth Euro title, the most of any country. The Euros are one of the sport's most prestigious competitions and the pinnacle of success for European national soccer teams.

The road to the 2016 final was anything but smooth for Portugal. Critics doubted them from the start. After a series of draws, they had a dramatic victory over Croatia, squeezed past Poland on penalties, and, through grit and determination, beat Wales 2-0 to reach the final match against France. The final match started with the intensity expected from any championship game. Every touch of the ball was fiercely contested, every pass made the crowd crane their necks, and Cristiano moved with his usual grace and power. He had an extra pep in his step thanks to his son, Ronaldo, Jr., who was watching in the stands. Over 600 *million* people watched the match at home on TV, and most fans (though probably not those in France) wanted to see number 7 win the first Euro championship in Portugal's history.

THE MOST VIEWED
4X!

NFL Super Bowl of all-time was Super Bowl LVIII, the 2024 matchup between the Kansas City Chiefs and San Francisco 49ers. That game had 123.4 million viewers. The 2016 Euro Final had enough viewers for *four* 2024 Super Bowls!

But then disaster struck. Twenty-five minutes into the game, Cristiano chased a loose ball and collided with France's Dimitri Payet. Cristiano crumbled to the ground and knew something was wrong right away. He clutched his knee and reality set in: he'd torn his ACL. He tried walking it off but couldn't stay on his feet. He was carried off the field on a stretcher along with the hopes and dreams of his country. It was the nightmare of 2004 all over again.

As Cristiano sat on the sidelines with his knee heavily wrapped, his determination never wavered. Since he couldn't help his fellow players physically, he became a coach, a motivator, and a leader. Limping up and down the sidelines, Cristiano clapped his hands, barked instructions, and inspired his teammates to push harder and dig deeper. In the 109th minute of extra time (extra minutes added to the total game time), Cristiano's encouragement paid off. Eder, a substitute brought on at the last minute, unleashed a shot from outside the box. Everyone held their breath as the ball sailed past the goalkeeper into the net. Against all odds, Portugal had won the European Championship.

Cristiano had waited 12 long years for this moment. Tears streamed down his face as he lifted the trophy high above his head. These weren't the same tears from 2004—now, they were tears of joy. This moment would help define Cristiano's legacy forever. But to truly understand how Cristiano got to this point, we need to go back to where it all began . . .

THE ACL

(or anterior cruciate ligament) is an important ligament in the knee that helps stabilize the joint by connecting the thigh and shin bones. Injuries can happen when this "rubber band" gets stretched too far or tears due to sudden stops, changes in direction, or jumps—the kinds of moves that often occur in sports like soccer, basketball, and football. Recovery from an ACL injury can take anywhere from six to nine months.

CHAPTER

THE BOY FROM MADEIRA

HUMBLE BEGINNINGS

It was the '80s—1985, to be exact. Kareem Abdul-Jabbar and Magic Johnson helped the Los Angeles Lakers beat Larry Bird's Boston Celtics; Nintendo had its North American launch; and the greatest time-travel movie ever (and future Broadway musical), *Back to the Future*, was the top movie in theaters. Despite many famous athletes being born this year—including Olympic swimmer Michael Phelps, Formula One driver Lewis Hamilton, and former pro soccer player Megan Rapinoe—the wide world of sports would forever be changed when the future

⚡ FAST FACTS ⚡
Portugal

- Portugal became a country in 1143, making it the oldest nation-state in Europe.
- Over half of the world's cork comes from Portugal. Next time you see someone open a bottle of wine, you can tell them the cork is probably from Portugal!
- The country is the birthplace of Ferdinand Magellan, the first explorer to circumnavigate the world.
- Livraria Bertrand is the world's oldest bookstore (open since 1732) and still operates throughout Portugal as a bookstore chain.
- In Nazaré, renowned surfer Sebastian Steudtner surfed the tallest wave ever recorded (93.73 feet, or 28.57 m)
- Bacalhau (dried and salted codfish) is Portugal's national dish, and Pastel de Nata (a vanilla custard tart) is its most famous dessert.

most followed person on Instagram (and one of the most decorated athletes of all time) was born during the second month of the year.

Cristiano Ronaldo dos Santos Aveiro was born February 5, 1985, to Maria Dolores dos Santos and José Dinis Aveiro. He was born in the São Pedro parish of Funchal, the capital city of the island of Madeira, which is located about 600 miles (966 km) off the coast of Portugal. Madeira is known for its famous wine, the Laurisilva forest, and their epic celebrations, which once gave them a Guinness World Record for the largest New Year's Eve fireworks display. While Madeira is a popular vacation spot with lush flowers, gorgeous beaches, and plenty of wealthy residents, Cristiano's story began very differently. His father was a city gardener, and his mother was a cook. Cristiano changed not only their lives and the lives of the people of Madeira, but would go on to change the sports world.

RONALD REAGAN was the 40th president of the United States and served two terms, from 1981 to 1989. Before he got into politics, Reagan was a Hollywood actor!

Ronald Reagan

37 USA

To fans all over the world, he may be known as CR7, El Bicho (The Bug), El Comandante (The Commander), or the GOAT (the Greatest Of All Time), but Cristiano's path to superstardom seemed destined from birth, thanks to a unique name given to him by his parents: Ronaldo. Where did that name come from? Ronald Reagan, who was his father's favorite actor and, at the time of Cristiano's birth, the President of the United States. Both of Cristiano's parents loved the films of Ronald Reagan and wanted to honor him by adding his name to their son. Who knew it would be chanted by millions one day?

The Origin of Soccer:
The Beautiful Game

About 2,000 years ago in ancient China, during the Han dynasty, people enjoyed a game that had many similarities to soccer, known as *cuju* (pronounced "tsu-joo"). This game resembled modern soccer in that it involved players kicking a leather ball stuffed with feathers and hair, trying to get it through a small hole in a net. In England in the 1800s, soccer began to take shape as we know it today. In 1863, the Football Association (FA) established the official rules, and "association football" was born. The game became the most popular sport in the history of the world, uniting fans from all over the world. All you need is a ball (or, in young Cristiano's case, rocks or rolled-up socks) and you can practice by yourself or start a game almost anywhere. This "beautiful game," as soccer legend Pelé called it, is a universal language connecting us all.

Little Cristiano grew up in a hillside village named Santo António with his older brother, Hugo, and two older sisters, Elma and Liliana Cátia. The family was very poor and lived in a small, tin-roofed house overlooking the ocean. The house was so small and cramped that their washing machine had to be placed on the roof. The house had just two rooms (all four siblings shared a bedroom) and a small bathroom the size of a closet. It seemed like the only light coming through the house was from the bedroom window or the holes in the ceiling. Cristiano was an unexpected blessing for his parents, who hadn't planned to have a fourth child. Even before he was born, Cristiano was defying the odds. Despite these challenging conditions, this tiny home by the ocean is where Cristiano's dreams took shape. Though his family barely had any money or the necessary room to live comfortably, little Cristiano only needed one thing to keep his spirits up and to let him dream big: a soccer ball.

THE BEAUTY OF
SOCCER

Cristiano's passion for soccer began at the extraordinarily young age of two. When most kids are just getting comfortable walking and learning to speak, Cristiano was already kicking a soccer ball on the patio. By age five Cristiano could run up and down the hill next to his home faster than most kids twice his age. As he grew older, other kids his age balanced their time between a variety of activities. But not Cristiano. Soccer consumed him.

SOCCER PLAYERS

run *a lot*. In a single game, they cover 7 to 10 miles (11 to 16 km)—that's like running across nearly 150 NFL fields in one 90-minute span. Midfielders run the most, while forwards like Cristiano focus more on quick sprints and scoring goals. Soccer is all about stamina, so make sure you keep your cardio up!

He skipped his studies (sometimes even dinner), neglected his chores, and ignored his homework, all in favor of spending hours practicing footwork and kicking the ball against the wall next to his home. (If your name isn't Cristiano Ronaldo, don't do this. It's important to keep up with all your responsibilities, whether that's homework, chores, spending time with family and friends, or helping out in your community.)

The steep hill outside was a training ground that strengthened his legs while practicing as he ran up and down to get his ball and was also a gateway to the local fields where he watched, learned, and trained, even at a young age.

The Hills Are Alive with Toboggans

The island of Madeira is full of hills. Every day, Cristiano would trek up and down them, playing with his soccer ball or finding pickup games to play with other kids. Visitors can experience the island's unique terrain by taking toboggan rides. This practice dates back to the early nineteenth century when locals would hop in traditional wicker basket sleds and fly down the streets, quickly traveling from Monte to Funchal. Today, with the help of two very skilled runners/navigators dressed in white and wearing straw hats, you can take a traditional toboggan ride down the hilly streets and reach speeds of up to 18 miles per hour (29 km/h)!

At school, Cristiano's teachers banned him from carrying around a soccer ball, so he rolled up his socks at recess to keep practicing and playing. His skills impressed all the older local kids who had initially denied him entry into their games. Once he flew around all of them, scoring goals, their opinion quickly shifted.

Cristiano may have found soccer (or perhaps soccer found him), but life at this time was far from easy for the future superstar. Soccer became his way of ignoring the poverty and darkness that surrounded him. His small village may have been surrounded by beauty, but at home his father, José, battled with a disease called alcoholism. Since returning from fighting in the Angolan Civil War, José struggled to hold down a steady job and provide for his family. Cristiano's mother, Maria, took on extra work cleaning houses to help make ends meet, often struggling to afford food for the family. Cristiano assumed that he'd grow up to be a fisherman on the island, and as a kid he earned a little extra money for his family by sweeping the hilly streets.

It was around this time that Cristiano vowed to never drink alcohol, as he saw firsthand its effects on his father and his family. Despite his struggles, José recognized the need for a strong, reliable figure in his son's life. They would often watch soccer matches together. José eventually got a job as a kit man for FC Andorinha, a local club, where he met Fernão Barros de Sousa, who he would eventually ask to become Cristiano's godfather.

Fernão, a local coach and mentor, provided the stability and guidance that Cristiano needed—and that José was

A KIT MAN, OR KIT MANAGER,

prepares and maintains a soccer team's equipment and uniforms (or kits) before, during, and after matches. They make sure all the players have the right gear, like jerseys, shorts, and cleats (or boots), and that everything is in top condition. They also organize and store the equipment and work closely with the coaching staff.

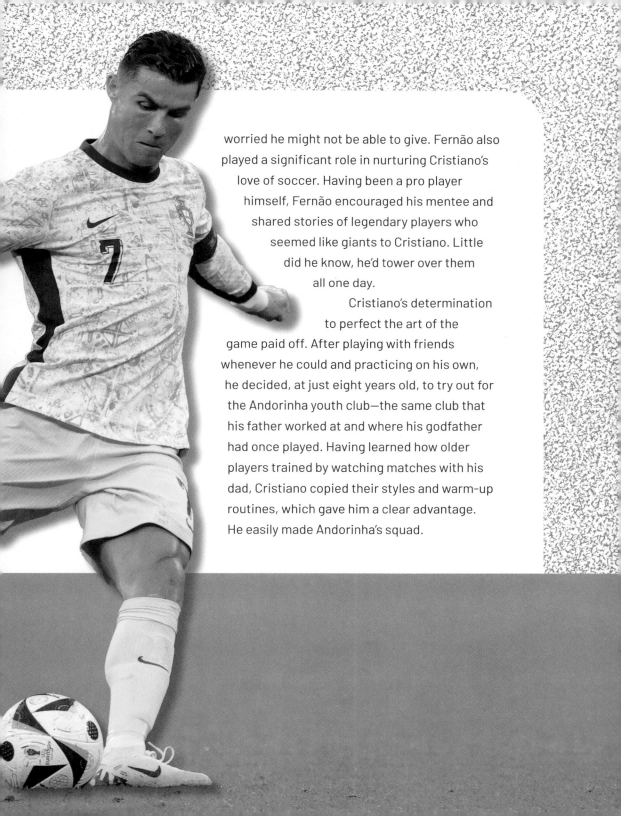

worried he might not be able to give. Fernão also played a significant role in nurturing Cristiano's love of soccer. Having been a pro player himself, Fernão encouraged his mentee and shared stories of legendary players who seemed like giants to Cristiano. Little did he know, he'd tower over them all one day.

Cristiano's determination to perfect the art of the game paid off. After playing with friends whenever he could and practicing on his own, he decided, at just eight years old, to try out for the Andorinha youth club—the same club that his father worked at and where his godfather had once played. Having learned how older players trained by watching matches with his dad, Cristiano copied their styles and warm-up routines, which gave him a clear advantage. He easily made Andorinha's squad.

PUTTING YOUR BEST FOOT FORWARD:
THE POSITIONS OF A SOCCER TEAM

Soccer positions are spread across four main categories: strikers or forwards, whose main job is to score goals; defenders, who specialize in stopping any goals; midfielders, who play both offense and defense and bridge the gap between defenders and forwards; and of course, goalkeepers, who are the last line of defense. The next couple of pages include some information about all eleven positions in soccer, plus a few famous players known for that position so you can watch highlights, model your game after them, and begin your own journey to soccer stardom!

GOALKEEPER ("GOALIE" OR "KEEPER")

Arguably the most important player on the pitch, their job is to protect the goal and stop the opposing team from scoring. The goalkeeper is the only player allowed to use their hands (as long as it's in the penalty area). Famous Goalies: Lev Yashin, Manuel Neuer, Gianluigi Buffon.

LEFT BACK

This defender, positioned on the left side of the defense, must block attacks from right wingers and help the team in forward movements. Famous Left Backs: Paolo Maldini, Paul Breitner, Jordi Alba.

CENTER BACK

This central defender plays in the middle of the defense. Their job is to stop strikers from scoring and to clear the ball from the defensive area. Famous Center Backs: Virgil van Dijk, Bobby Moore, Daniel Passarella.

SWEEPER (LIBERO)

With no specific opponent to follow, the sweeper is a versatile center back who freely moves around the defense to sweep up loose balls that get past the defenders. Famous Sweepers: Rafael Márquez, Franz Beckenbauer, Franco Baresi.

RIGHT BACK

This defender, positioned on the right side of the defense, must stop attacks from left wingers on the opposing team and assist in the offense. Famous Right Backs: Cafu, Gary Neville, Trent Alexander-Arnold.

LEFT MIDFIELDER (LEFT WINGER)

This midfielder plays on the left side of the field. They deliver crosses and passes to the forwards and help with defensive strategy. **Famous Left Wingers: Christian Pulisic, Ronaldhino, Neymar.**

DEFENSIVE MIDFIELDER (CENTRAL DEFENSIVE MIDFIELDER)

This midfielder plays directly in front of all the defenders. They protect the defense by stopping attacks from the other team and help move the ball upfield. **Famous Defensive Midfielders: Claude Makélélé, Didier Deschamps, Roy Keane.**

RIGHT MIDFIELDER (RING WINGER)

This midfielder plays on the right side of the field. They support both the defense and attacking the goal and are responsible for delivering crosses into the penalty area. **Famous Right Wingers: David Beckham, Luis Figo, George Best.**

ATTACKING MIDFIELDER (CENTRAL ATTACKING MIDFIELDER)

Playing close to the forwards, the attacking midfielder focuses on creating scoring opportunities with key passes and assists to the strikers and can even score goals themselves. Famous Attacking Midfielders: Diego Maradona, Zinedine Zidane, Lionel Messi.

CENTER MIDFIELDER

This midfielder is very involved in overall strategy by controlling the game from the middle of the field. They take part in both attacking and defending and distribute the ball to help maintain possession. Famous Center Midfielders: Lothar Matthaus, Luka Modrić, Xavi.

STRIKER (FORWARD)

Strikers have one job: score goals. They play near the opponent's goal and look for opportunities to score or help their teammates score. Famous Strikers: Cristiano Ronaldo, Pelé, Erling Haaland.

Even at a young age, Cristiano had his insatiable need to win at all costs. If it meant he scored all the goals, so be it. But with his competitiveness came strong emotions. Despite easily running around all his teammates, when Cristiano didn't get the ball or missed a goal or didn't like the way he was tackled, he often cried. His first nickname was born: "Crybaby."

ATHLETES EXPRESS

their emotions in all kinds of ways, both on and off the field. Some of the world's most gifted sports stars aren't afraid to wear their hearts on their sleeves. This raw emotion can come in many forms, like confidence or trash-talking (from stars like Muhammed Ali, Larry Bird, Deion Sanders); fiery passion (Serena Williams, Tom Brady, Kobe Bryant), and crying tears of joy or pain during the biggest moments of their careers (Michael Jordan, Cristiano Ronaldo, Roger Federer).

For Cristiano to become the legend we all know and love today, there was one skill he had to learn to be successful: teamwork. To win in soccer, as with every team sport, everyone must work together. Cristiano would learn this valuable skill as he got older.

By age 10, Cristiano was getting bigger and faster each day he trained and played. He was so fast and elusive, buzzing across the pitch around players, that he earned a new nickname: *Abelhinha*, or Little Bee. He became unstoppable on offense and defense and was already an all-around player. He scored three goals during one game, putting his team up 3-0 by halftime. After he got injured and couldn't play the rest of the game, his team ended up losing 4–3. Cristiano began to dominate his league. It was clear to him, his family, his godfather, and the island of Madeira that he was a standout that would make any team better. An even bigger club, Clube Desportivo Nacional (known as Nacional), took notice.

The head of the youth program at Nacional heard of a fantastic player at Andorinha and sent a scout to check him out. That scout was none other than Cristiano's godfather, Fernão, who had no idea he was sent to scout his godson! Fernão saw immediately that Cristiano had grown as a player (despite being undersized and malnourished), and went to Cristiano's mother to get her approval to let him move clubs. Next came the transaction fee, which is paid any time a player changes clubs. In this case, it was far from the millions of dollars Cristiano would get in the future. And what did it cost? Nacional bought Cristiano from Andorinha for twenty soccer balls and two sets of kits!

Nacional was Cristiano's biggest test. To keep his dreams alive, he needed to prove he was the best player on the pitch. At just 10 years old, Cristiano felt a lot of pressure to impress his new coaches. The next two years would be crucial to the story of Cristiano Ronaldo—and he was ready to write the first chapter.

Soccer Speak:
A GLOSSARY

Whether you call it soccer, football, or *fútbol*, it's the same game with the same rules. You probably already know basic soccer terms like **shoot** (kick the ball toward the goal), **save** (prevent a goal from being scored), **pass** (get the ball to your teammate), and **goal** (when a ball goes into the net and earns a point). Learn the additional terms below before you lace up for your next practice!

Cap: A player earns a "cap" when they represent their country in an international match. If a player has 25 caps, it means they have played 25 times or made 25 appearances for their country.

AS OF 2024, Cristiano has 217 caps. He became the first player to reach 200 international appearances when Portugal played Iceland in June 2023. **217**

Corner Kick: When the ball goes out of play over the goal line but doesn't cross into the net, a player kicks it from the corner of the field to create a scoring opportunity for their team.

Cross: This is a kick from the side of the field to the middle, where teammates can try to score.

Dribbling: Just like basketball, dribbling in soccer involves moving the ball up the field—although in soccer, you do it by tapping it with your feet while running. Cristiano is one of the best dribblers in the game and is often called "twinkle toes" because of his fast and efficient dribbling.

Free Kick: This kick is awarded to a team after a foul. The fouled team gets a chance to either shoot the ball or pass it without interference.

Offside: If a player is closer to the goal than the second-to-last defender when the ball is passed, they are offside. Don't worry if it takes time to get the hang of this one—it's a tricky rule that some people still argue about!

Penalty Kick: When a player is fouled inside the penalty area, they get this special kick. The fouled player faces off against the goalie, shooting toward the net from twelve yards away.

Promotion: A team is promoted when they perform well enough to move up to a higher league starting the next season.

Relegation: When a team doesn't perform well, they are dropped (or relegated) to a lower division for the next season.

Throw-In: When the ball goes out of play over a sideline, a player can throw it back into the field from behind their head using both hands.

CHAPTER

2

A TRUE PROFESSIONAL

MOVING
UP

Upon arriving at C.D. Nacional, Cristiano was surprised to learn that pretty much everyone knew who he was. They could see he had a magic touch with a soccer ball, but what really set him apart was the fact that, unlike most players his age, he could shoot and pass with equal power and precision using either foot. This skill, along with shooting spectacular goals, made him a nightmare for defenders. They never knew which way he would go—and it didn't matter anyway, because whatever angle he was at, he was always in striking distance.

Ambidexterity

(or being ambidextrous) is the ability to use both the right and left hands—or right and left feet—with equal skill. Here are some other famous ambidextrous people:

- **Leonardo da Vinci:** Artist and inventor known for the *Mona Lisa* and *The Last Supper*.

- **Albert Einstein:** Theoretical physicist famous for developing the theory of relativity.

- **Benjamin Franklin:** Founding Father of the United States, inventor, writer, and statesman.

- **Kobe Bryant:** Five-time NBA champion of the Los Angeles Lakers.

- **Maria Sharapova:** Former number-one-ranked Russian tennis champion and Olympic medalist.

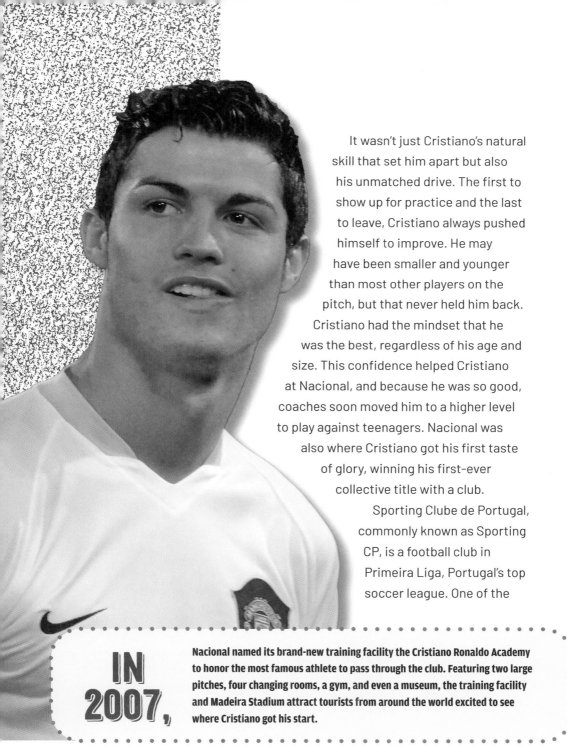

It wasn't just Cristiano's natural skill that set him apart but also his unmatched drive. The first to show up for practice and the last to leave, Cristiano always pushed himself to improve. He may have been smaller and younger than most other players on the pitch, but that never held him back. Cristiano had the mindset that he was the best, regardless of his age and size. This confidence helped Cristiano at Nacional, and because he was so good, coaches soon moved him to a higher level to play against teenagers. Nacional was also where Cristiano got his first taste of glory, winning his first-ever collective title with a club.

Sporting Clube de Portugal, commonly known as Sporting CP, is a football club in Primeira Liga, Portugal's top soccer league. One of the

IN 2007, Nacional named its brand-new training facility the Cristiano Ronaldo Academy to honor the most famous athlete to pass through the club. Featuring two large pitches, four changing rooms, a gym, and even a museum, the training facility and Madeira Stadium attract tourists from around the world excited to see where Cristiano got his start.

31

premier teams in the league, Sporting CP has won nineteen championships since being founded in 1906. Along with teams Benfica and Porto, it is one of "The Big Three"—the most powerful clubs in the entire country. When 12-year-old Cristiano got a call that Sporting CP wanted him to try out for their youth program, it was the best news he had ever received. Cristiano's godfather, Fernão, assisted with the connection, stepping up once more in his godson's life and bragging to all his contacts in Lisbon—Portugal's capital and home to Sporting CP—just how good Cristiano was. In those

days, scouting wasn't about analytics and draft reports; it was more about gut feelings after seeing a player in person.

Sporting CP flew Cristiano out for a tryout. It was the first time Cristiano had ever been on a plane and the first time he had ever left home alone. But there was no time for nerves. Cristiano's performance at this tryout would decide if he was good enough for the pros.

IN 1966, THE WORLD CUP

trophy was stolen in England—but a scrappy dog named Pickles became a national hero after finding the trophy wrapped in newspaper while sniffing a bush. Pickles was named Dog of the Year, starred in a movie, and got free food for a year!

WOLFGANG AMADEUS MOZART,

an Austrian composer born in 1756, started creating music as a child. He composed his first piece of music at age 5 and his first opera by age 12. In his lifetime, he composed over 600 works.

During Cristiano's tryout, even the older players on the top team stopped their workouts and practices to watch him play. Coach Aurélio Pereira saw Cristiano as an artist (not yet an athlete), comparing him to Mozart. Both the footballer and the composer had natural talent at young ages, but the hours of work they put in behind the scenes made them elite.

After the tryout, Sporting CP had seen enough. They knew that Cristiano was a generational talent and had to have him. They offered him about $2,000 to join their youth program—but there was a catch. To join this prestigious club, Cristiano would have to leave his home and family and move to Lisbon, over 600 miles (966 km) away. Sporting CP was one of the biggest clubs in all of Portugal, and their youth program was his best shot at growing as a player. Cristiano knew what he had to do. After discussing with his family (and hearing encouragement from his mother, his biggest supporter), Cristiano bravely decided to chase his dreams.

LIFE IN
LISBON

Lisbon was bigger, louder, and far from the quiet, familiar streets of island life on Madeira. Cristiano felt alone and missed his family terribly, especially his mom. Like many countries, different areas of Portugal have different accents, and Cristiano had a very thick Madeiran accent that set him apart from the other boys at the academy. They even teased him for it, which made him feel out of place.

But Cristiano reminded himself of why he was in Lisbon: to become the best soccer player in the world. It didn't matter if people laughed at his accent or doubted his abilities or if he felt smaller and weaker than some of the other players—he was determined to succeed. Cristiano threw himself into training, working out more to get bigger and stronger and practicing harder than ever.

But when he was just 15 years old and far from home, Cristiano faced his biggest challenge yet. He began having a strange pounding sensation in his chest during training that didn't go away. Cristiano saw a doctor and was diagnosed with tachycardia, or a racing heart. This condition could have ended his dreams of playing soccer. Luckily, it didn't! Doctors recommended a special surgery using a laser. With his mother by his side, Cristiano underwent the procedure in the morning and returned home that same afternoon. His mother said that she believed he was even faster after the procedure!

TACHYCARDIA is when the heart beats irregularly or faster than normal (more than 100 beats per minute, even at rest). It's normal for your heart to beat faster while playing soccer or engaging in any physical activity. However, if your heart rate remains high during rest and is accompanied by chest pain, dizziness, or shortness of breath, it's time to see a doctor, just like Cristiano did.

Following his heart surgery, Cristiano's rise at Sporting CP was nothing short of meteoric. Thanks to his coaches, he learned a very important lesson: the ball was not just his. Cristiano was coached to transform from an *individual* player to a *team* player. With this new mindset, Cristiano was promoted to the first team just one year later, at age 16. In fact, he moved up from the under-16 team to the under-17 team, the under-18 team, the B team, and all the way to the first team within a single season. That's like a high school sophomore joining the JV basketball team, moving up to varsity, starting at a big college, getting drafted to the NBA, and then starting in the NBA—all within the same year!

On October 7, 2002, shortly after making his Primeira Liga debut with the first team, Cristiano scored his first goal against Moreirense. He scored two goals in that game, for a 3–0 win.

Not long after newspapers wrote about this young sensation, scouts from across Europe and the biggest soccer leagues in the world made special trips to Portugal. Teams from England's Premier League, including Arsenal, Liverpool, and Manchester United, were interested in Cristiano. And he wasn't even 18 yet! For Cristiano, the idea of moving to England (where soccer isn't just a game—it's practically a religion) was both exciting and daunting, but necessary if he was going to be the best.

The Big FIVE

When it comes to professional soccer, the "Big Five" leagues aren't just where the world's best players compete—they're home to jaw-dropping goals, legendary rivalries, incredible stories, and dramatic last-minute victories watched and loved by millions of fans from around the world. The Big Five are:

1. **English Premier League (EPL) (England)**
   Most popular teams: Manchester United, Chelsea, Manchester City, Liverpool, Arsenal
   Most recent champion: Manchester City (2023-24)

2. **La Liga (Spain)**
   Most popular teams: Real Madrid, Barcelona, Atlético Madrid, Valencia, Athletic Club
   Most recent champion: Real Madrid (2023-24)

3. **Bundesliga (Germany)**
   Most popular teams: Bayern Munich, Dortmund, Leipzig, Bayer Leverkusen, Mönchengladbach
   Most recent champion: Bayer Leverkusen (2023-24)

4. **Serie A (Italy)**
   Most Ppopular teams: Juventus, AC Milan, Inter Milan, AS Roma, SSC Napoli
   Most recent champion: Inter Milan (2023-24)

5. **Ligue 1 (France)**
   Most popular teams: Paris Saint-Germain (PSG), Marseille, Lyon, Monaco, Lille
   Most recent champion: Paris Saint-Germain (2023-24)

On August 6, 2003, Sporting Lisbon played an exhibition match against Manchester United, the most famous football club in the world. Cristiano wasn't even supposed to start that game. Still, when a spot opened after a player transferred to Barcelona, he took the field. During the match, Cristiano didn't just have the confidence of an 18-year-old but the swagger of a longtime pro as he fearlessly took on some of the best players in the world. His first target was United right back **John O'Shea**. Using his blistering speed and a combination of dribbles and stepovers, Cristiano made O'Shea look like an amateur. Famed Manchester United coach Sir Alex Ferguson said in his autobiography that Cristiano left O'Shea with a "look of pain and bewilderment across his face," and O'Shea's teammates, such as Roy Keane (the basis for Roy Kent on *Ted Lasso*), said he had to see the doctor at halftime because he was having dizzy spells.

A STEPOVER

is an offensive dribbling move in which a player fakes a change in direction to deceive a defender by quickly circling their foot around the ball multiple times. The intent is to make the defender commit to one direction, with the offensive player then going the other way.

Manchester United may be nicknamed the Red Devils, but Cristiano left them all seeing red that day. The entire team noticed and urged Coach Ferguson to sign Cristiano immediately. Coach Ferguson was already in talks with Sporting CP about doing exactly that. After the match, he told Cristiano, "I want you now." Five days later, Manchester United secured Cristiano for £12.24 million (almost $16 million), making him the highest-paid teenager in British football history!

Manchester United

- Formed in 1878 as Newton Heath LYR Football Club (originally wearing green and gold); in 1902 changed their name to Manchester United and adopted their now-famous red jerseys.

- Most successful club in English football history, with twenty English league titles.

- Play matches at **Old Trafford** (opened in 1910), nicknamed the "Theatre of Dreams." Its seating capacity is over 74,000, second only to Wembley Stadium's 90,000 seats.

- Sir Alex Ferguson managed the team from 1986 to 2013 and is regarded as one of the best football managers of all time. During his tenure, United won 13 Premier League titles, five FA Cups, and two Champions League trophies.

- The official mascot is Fred the Red, a red devil, who represents one of the largest fan bases in sports.

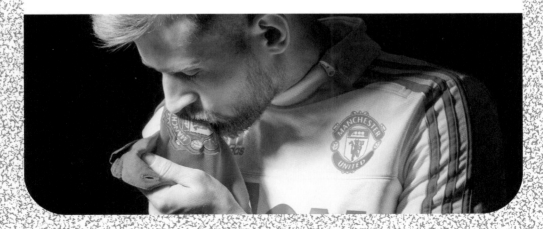

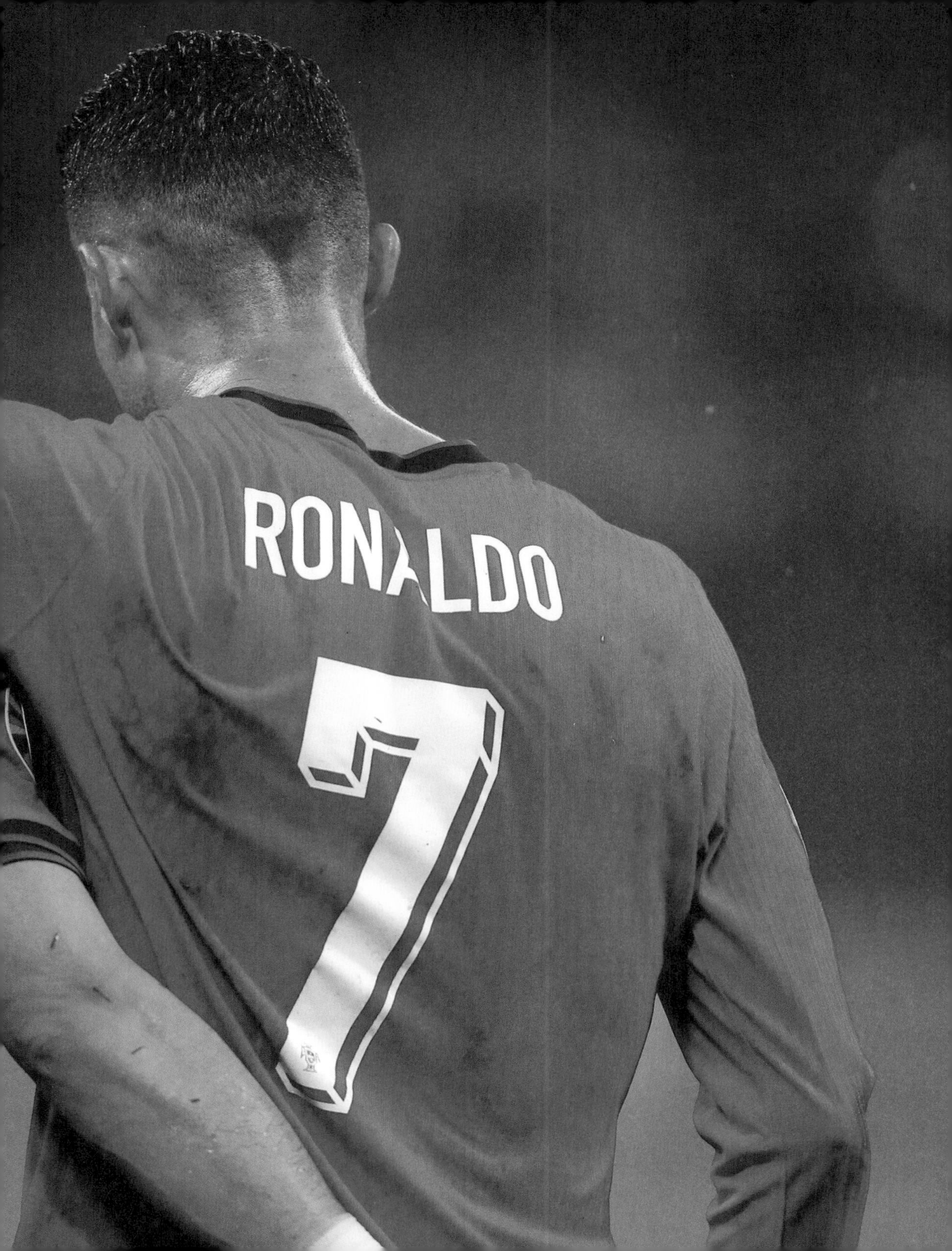
RONALDO
7

BECOMING A
RED DEVIL

Arriving in Manchester in 2003, it was a dream come true for Cristiano. This wasn't some run-of-the-mill football club—it was one of the most prestigious in the world with a rich history of winning, especially under the guidance of its legendary coach, Sir Alex Ferguson. Cristiano knew he was stepping into a footballing powerhouse. Not only that, he was now playing in a country with a completely different language, culture, and style of soccer. Despite the weight of these expectations on his young shoulders, he was ready to prove he could thrive in such elite company.

Coach Ferguson also saw his greatness. When Cristiano asked for his typical number 28, he was denied. Coach Ferguson insisted he wear number 7. Only the greatest players in Manchester United history get to wear the legendary number 7. Cristiano embraced it, determined to add his name to that storied lineage.

OTHER FAMOUS
Manchester United players who have donned number 7 include Eric Cantona, George Best, David Beckham, and Bryan Robson. Some of the most famous players in other sports have also worn number 7: Hall of Fame quarterback John Elway, Hall of Fame basketball player "Pistol" Pete Maravich, and Hall of Fame baseball player Mickey Mantle.

Playing in the Premier League didn't come as easily to Cristiano. It was faster, more physical, and relentless, unlike anything he had experienced. But Cristiano had the work ethic to take it on, working and training even harder and meeting every challenge head-on. His first season showed him that he still wasn't strong enough to withstand the league's tough defenses and physical play. He spent many hours in the gym, and his coaches remember him continuing to train alone (like he had late at night in Portugal) long after his teammates had left, practicing his free kicks and perfecting his dribbling. By the end of his first season, Cristiano was making progress—he had four goals and four assists in 29 appearances. He quickly became a fan favorite. The end of the season saw the Red Devils finish in third place, but Cristiano wasn't satisfied.

When the team entered the FA Cup, they made it to the final against Millwall. In the 44th minute, Cristiano scored the opening goal with a **header**, which would become a signature move. His early heroics helped United secure a 3-0 win, and Cristiano got to hold his first professional trophy. Before he could process the great end to his first season in the big leagues, another monumental invitation came his way. Though it would give him his first taste of disappointment, it would only make him stronger.

THE FA CUP

The Football Association Challenge Cup, known as the FA Cup, is the oldest soccer competition in the world. Teams from all over England, big and small alike, compete in a knockout-style tournament (meaning if you lose, you're out), which can lead to big underdog victories and upsets. The tournament takes place during the regular season, adding another level of difficulty.

CHAPTER

ON THE
WORLD STAGE

PLAYING FOR HIS
COUNTRY

—

On August 20, 2003, Ronaldo achieved a lifelong dream: wearing Portugal's iconic red and green jersey. He was about to earn his first cap (appearance for a national team) in a match against Kazakhstan. This was Cristiano's chance to show the world—not just England or Portugal—what he could do.

Cristiano entered the game as a substitute. He didn't score a goal, but the team won the match 1–0. Then, less than a year after this debut, his true test arrived: Euro 2004, which would take place *in* Portugal. Could a 19-year-old handle the weight of the nation's expectations?

Club vs. Country

There are two types of professional soccer teams: club and national.

A **club team** (like Manchester United in the Premier League) is composed of players from around the world who sign contracts to play in that specific league. They can be transferred from team to team within the league and can earn large salaries.

A **national team** (like Portugal) is made up of players who are citizens of that specific country. Each nation has teams of players at different age levels. National teams compete in international competitions like the World Cup and Euros.

The tournament kicked off with Cristiano and Portugal taking on Greece in an intense game that saw Portugal trailing Greece 2–0. But Cristiano never gave up. He leaped in the air and headed a ball into the back of the net. It was his first goal for Portugal on the international stage. Though the goal came too late and Portugal lost 2–1, Cristiano's skills helped Portugal fight to the tournament's final game. And who was their opponent? Greece—*again*. Heading into the Euros, Greece had stood at 150-1 odds. Still, they went on an incredible winning run, beating the defending champions, France, on their way to the final. That final game was hard-fought, and Greece pulled off the unthinkable to beat Portugal 1–0. The defeat would stay with Cristiano for over a decade, driving him to seek redemption on the Euro stage.

GREECE only scored seven goals in the entire 2004 Euro tournament but still won the trophy. Their big upset was thanks to solid defense and sound strategy that took them from underdogs to champions.

In the 2004–05 season with Manchester United, Cristiano showed glimpses of the player he would become—but he wasn't there yet. He was still finding his footing and his confidence. Still, he scored nine goals across all competitions, and Manchester United finished third in the Premier League.

But the most devastating hit of 2005 came when Cristiano was with Portugal, getting ready for a match against Russia. His coach, Felipe Scolari, got the news that Cristiano's father, José, had passed away due to liver failure. No one knew how to tell Cristiano, so Scolari did it himself, having lost a parent not long before. Cristiano had hoped his father would see his success, but that opportunity was now gone.

THE HIGHEST SOCCER SCORE

ever recorded was 149-0. On October 31, 2002, Madagascar's SO l'Emyrne (SOE) intentionally scored 149 own goals (against themselves) while facing off with rivals AS Adema. Why in the world did they do this? SOE was protesting decisions by the referees from a previous game. The original record belonged to Bon Accord Football Club, who once lost 36-0 to Arbroath in the first round of the Scottish Cup in 1885.

As Cristiano worked toward improving every day, he set his sights on the 2006 FIFA World Cup, which would be held in Germany. During the tournament's group stage—in which teams are divided into eight groups and play several matches until the top two teams in each group (16 total) advance to a single-elimination knockout stage—Cristiano and Portugal had a memorable match against Iran. In the eightieth minute, Cristiano stepped up to take a penalty kick. He took a deep breath, waited for the referee to signal his start, then smashed the ball into the back of the net. He dropped to his knees and let out a scream of happiness. At just 21 years and 132 days old, Ronaldo became the youngest Portuguese player to score a goal in a World Cup match. He was named Man of the Match three times throughout the tournament, and Portugal made it to the semifinals, their best year since 1966. Unfortunately, a strong French team crushed their World Cup glory and Portugal finished fourth in the tournament.

What in the World is the World Cup?

The World Cup is the biggest and most watched sporting event on the planet. Organized by Fédération Internationale de Football Association (FIFA), this global soccer tournament is held every four years. It brings together 32 of the best national teams to compete for soccer's ultimate championship. Starting in 2026, the tournament will be expanded to 48 teams.

The inaugural World Cup was held in 1930 in Uruguay. It has occurred every four years since (except 1942 and 1946, due to World War II) in different locations around the world. The tournament lasts about a month and features 64 matches, with billions of people tuning in.

Top 3
World Cup Winning Countries

1. Brazil
5 titles (1958, 1962, 1970, 1994, 2002)

2. Germany
4 titles (1954, 1974, 1990, 2014)

3. Italy
4 titles (1934, 1938, 1982, 2006)

After the World Cup, Cristiano returned as a different player. He had been through hardships on and off the field. He was no longer the skinny kid who defenders could easily tackle and block. He was stronger, more muscular, and had a renewed focus.

This time also marked the start of Cristiano's obsession with his physical fitness. He understood that to be the best, he had to train like the best. Under the guidance of Sir Alex Ferguson, Cristiano developed into a leader alongside Wayne Rooney, considered one of the greatest English soccer players of all time and record holder for the most goals at Manchester United with 183. Together, Cristiano and Rooney were an

Legendary Dynamic Duos in Sports

- **Babe Ruth** and **Lou Gehrig** (New York Yankees; MLB)
- **Wayne Gretzky** and **Mark Messier** (Edmonton Oilers; NHL)
- **Steph Curry** and **Klay Thompson** (Golden State Warriors, NBA)
- **Tom Brady** and **Rob Gronkowski** (New England Patriots; NFL)
- **Xavi Hernandez** and **Andres Iniesta** (FC Barcelona; La Liga)

unstoppable two-pronged attack, striking fear into the hearts of defenders across Europe.

The most significant change aside from Cristiano's physique was that he passed more. He knew when to dribble and when to pass, and this team-forward mentality not only helped the squad be more well-rounded but also took the pressure off Cristiano to do everything. This new squad, which put team over self and was brilliantly led by Cristiano and Rooney, would soon go on a tear through the Premier League, for which no one was ready.

The Red Devils went on a historic run during the 2007-08 season, winning *three* major trophies—Premier League, UEFA Champions League, FA Community Shield—in that one season. Not only that, Cristiano helped Manchester United win two more consecutive Premier League titles. From 2007 to 2009, Manchester United, and specifically Cristiano, were unstoppable. He scored forty-two goals in all competitions during the 2007-08 season.

In 2008, Cristiano was recognized as the best footballer in the world when he received the famous Ballon d'Or award. He was the first Manchester United player to win it since George Best in 1968.

The Ballon d'Or
Soccer's Most Prestigious Prize

The Ballon d'Or is given every year to the best soccer player in the world, recognizing their hard work, incredible skills, and impact on the game.

Top Ballon d'Or Winners

1. **Lionel Messi** (Argentina): 8 awards (2009, 2010, 2011, 2012, 2015, 2019, 2021, 2023)
2. **Cristiano Ronaldo** (Portugal): 5 awards (2008, 2013, 2014, 2016, 2017)
3. **Michel Platini** (France): 3 awards (1983, 1984, 1985)
4. **Johan Cruyff** (Netherlands): 3 awards (1971, 1973, 1974)
5. **Marco van Basten** (Netherlands): 3 awards (1988, 1989, 1992)

FAST FACTS

- **Lionel Messi** holds the record for most wins (8) and is the only player to win the award with three different teams.
- **Cristiano** has the most nominations ever (18).
- The first winner was **Stanley Matthews**, who is also the oldest player to win the award at 41 years old.
- **Lev Yashin** from the Soviet Union is the only goalkeeper to ever win the award.
- **George Weah** from Liberia in 1995 became the first African player to win the award.

THE REAL MADRID ERA

In 2009, Cristiano transferred to Real Madrid, the most famous and prestigious soccer club in the world, located in Spain. His transfer fee was huge—£80 million (about $131 million), which was a world record at the time. Like David Beckham before him, Cristiano had become a global superstar who needed to take his talents to new heights. As he said goodbye to the Manchester United fans who had supported him for six years, an exciting new chapter began.

When Cristiano arrived in Madrid, he was treated like a king. Over 80,000 fans packed into Santiago Bernabéu Stadium each match to witness a spectacle like no other. Once more, Cristiano was under immense pressure, but he started with a bang. His time at Real Madrid was filled with endless success, starting that first season with 33 goals in just 35 matches. Cristiano also helped his team win multiple UEFA Champions League titles, including three consecutive titles from 2016 to 2018. That success made him the only player in soccer history to three-peat both the Premier League and the UEFA Champions League.

CRISTIANO'S

iconic goal celebration, known as the "Si!" celebration, has become a global symbol of his goal-scoring skills. After scoring, Cristiano runs and twirls his fingers to wind up the crowd, then performs a high leap, spins midair, and lands with his arms and legs outstretched, shouting "Si!"—which means "Yes!" in Spanish.

In 2013, five years after receiving his first Ballon d'Or award, Cristiano was invited back to the stage to accept another one commemorating his play in Spain. This one was extra special, as Cristiano's three-year-old son, Cristiano, Jr., joined him on stage. Cristiano tearfully thanked his coaches, teammates, mother, and family for the honor. Following this trophy, Cristiano won three more during his time at Real Madrid and became their all-time leading goal scorer.

But Cristiano's time in La Liga wasn't really about the awards, the championships, or the personal achievements—it was about the birth of the greatest rivalry and GOAT debate soccer has ever known: between Cristiano, the confident showman with his razzle-dazzle, and Lionel Messi, a player on Barcelona (another La Liga team), a quiet genius who calculates every move.

Introducing Lionel Messi
Five Fun Facts

1. Upon his birth in Rosario, Argentina, Messi was diagnosed with a growth hormone deficiency. Barcelona's famed La Masia Academy covered his medical treatment and nurtured his rise to greatness.
2. In 2004, when he was just 17, Messi debuted for Barcelona and became their all-time leading scorer with 672 goals. He also holds the record for most goals in La Liga with 474.
3. Messi helped his home country of Argentina win the FIFA World Cup in 2022.
4. Messi was nicknamed "La Pulga," or "The Flea," because of his small 5-foot, 7-inch frame, which, in addition to his speed and agility, allows him to dart between defenders.
5. Messi shocked the world in 2023 by joining Inter Miami CF in the MLS under team owner David Beckham.

EL CLÁSICO

Any time Real Madrid and Barcelona face off, it's one of the biggest matches in sports. That's why this incredible matchup has its own nickname: "El Clásico," or the Classic.

So, who is the better player, Cristiano Ronaldo or Lionel Messi? Here are stats from their head-to-head matchups and overall numbers to help you decide:

El Clásico

Goals: Cristiano (18), Messi (26)

Assists: Cristiano (1), Messi (14)

Wins: Cristiano (9), Messi (19)

Titles: Cristiano (2), Messi (4)

Overall Stats
(All-Time as of December 2024)

Goals: Cristiano (916), Messi (850)

Assists: Cristiano (256), Messi (379)

International Goals:
Cristiano (135), Messi (112)

Champions League Titles: Cristiano (5), Messi (4)

League Titles: Cristiano (7), Messi (12)

Ballon d'Or: Cristiano (5), Messi (8)

Euro: Cristiano (1), Messi (0)

World Cup:
Cristiano (0), Messi (1)

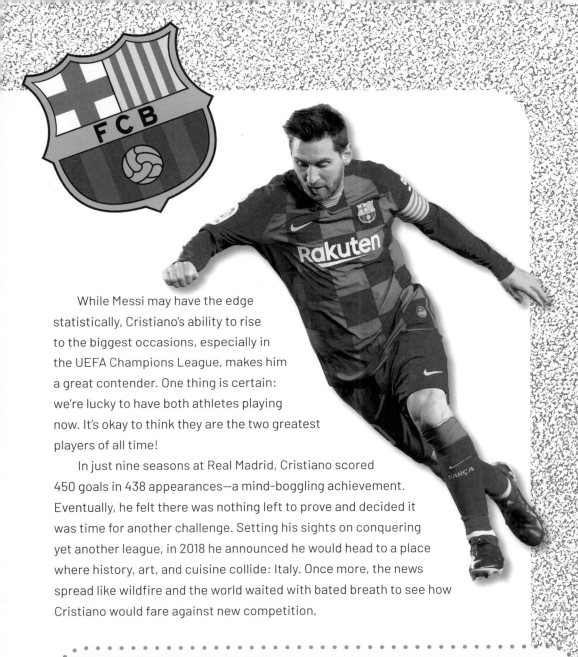

While Messi may have the edge statistically, Cristiano's ability to rise to the biggest occasions, especially in the UEFA Champions League, makes him a great contender. One thing is certain: we're lucky to have both athletes playing now. It's okay to think they are the two greatest players of all time!

In just nine seasons at Real Madrid, Cristiano scored 450 goals in 438 appearances—a mind-boggling achievement. Eventually, he felt there was nothing left to prove and decided it was time for another challenge. Setting his sights on conquering yet another league, in 2018 he announced he would head to a place where history, art, and cuisine collide: Italy. Once more, the news spread like wildfire and the world waited with bated breath to see how Cristiano would fare against new competition.

WOULD YOU RATHER

have Messi's magical dribbling abilities and vision around the field or Cristiano's athleticism and goal-scoring prowess?

CHAPTER

NEW TEAMS

BLACK AND WHITE

n July 2018, Cristiano's sleek private jet touched down in Turin, Italy. He was 33 years old, an age when most players consider winding down or are already retired. But Cristiano was about to embark on a new chapter. Exiting the plane with his mother and girlfriend, Cristiano was poised to conquer the best league in all of Italy: Serie A, known for solid defenses and defenders being notoriously difficult on strikers. The entire country was excited that the world's premiere striker was now with them—and not against them.

Cristiano was joining Juventus, founded in 1897 by a group of grammar students and known affectionately as "the Old Lady" of Italian football. Juventus paid Cristiano a massive £116 million (about $128 million) transfer fee, the largest amount ever paid for a player over 30. It was also a statement from Juventus that they didn't just want to dominate other Italian clubs, they wanted to dominate all of Europe—and Cristiano was the one to help them do it.

Ronaldo's Flying Mansion

Cristiano cruises through the skies in serious style with his **Gulfstream G650**, a $73 million jet that's practically a mansion in the air. It has bedrooms, a bathroom, a spacious cabin, reclining seats, and multipurpose desks, perfect for traveling with family and special guests. It can carry up to 19 passengers and has room for 100 pieces of luggage. This jet also has a top speed of just under the speed of sound!

! TOTALLY AWESOME FACTS !

ITALY

- Italy has 60 **UNESCO** World Heritage Sites (places with "cultural and natural heritage around the world considered to be of outstanding value to humanity")—more than any other country.

- **Venice** is a marvel of engineering, with a city center without roads for cars, only canals for boats and gondolas. It was built on 118 small islands connected by over 400 bridges.

- Italy is the birthplace of pizza! Invented in Naples in 1189, legend has it that the classic **Margherita pizza** is named after former Queen of Italy, Margherita of Savoy, and the three ingredients—tomato, mozzarella, and basil—are meant to correspond to the colors of the Italian flag.

- Italy is home to the smallest country in the world, Vatican City, where the Pope lives. Tucked within the city of Rome, you can walk around this tiny country in just one hour.

- The famous **Leaning Tower of Pisa** took a whopping 199 years to complete. Its iconic lean was caused by the uneven settling of the building's foundation.

UNESCO

JUVENTUS

In Cristiano's first few practices with Juventus, he realized the difference in their style of soccer. It was slower and more methodical, but just as intense. Every move had to be calculated, which took a bit of getting used to. In his first season, he scored 28 goals in all competitions and helped Juventus secure their eighth consecutive Serie A title. That win also made him the first player to win domestic titles in England, Spain, and Italy. TV ratings skyrocketed and the entire league's profile received a huge boost. Stadiums were packed any time Juventus came to town.

IF YOU COULD see any athlete (living or dead) perform, who would it be and why?

With so many memorable moments of Cristiano's time with Juventus, one stands (or leaps) above the rest. One of his most spectacular goals ever came in December 2019 in a match against Sampdoria. As a cross came in from the left, Cristiano ran and leaped into the air. Like a superhero, his body seemed suspended in time and he floated higher than the crossbar at nearly 8.3 feet (2.5 m), almost on the defender's shoulders, and ultimately found the ball with his head to knock in the winning goal. The stadium erupted in disbelief and awe. This header was a testament to Cristiano's longevity as a superstar and his undeniable athleticism.

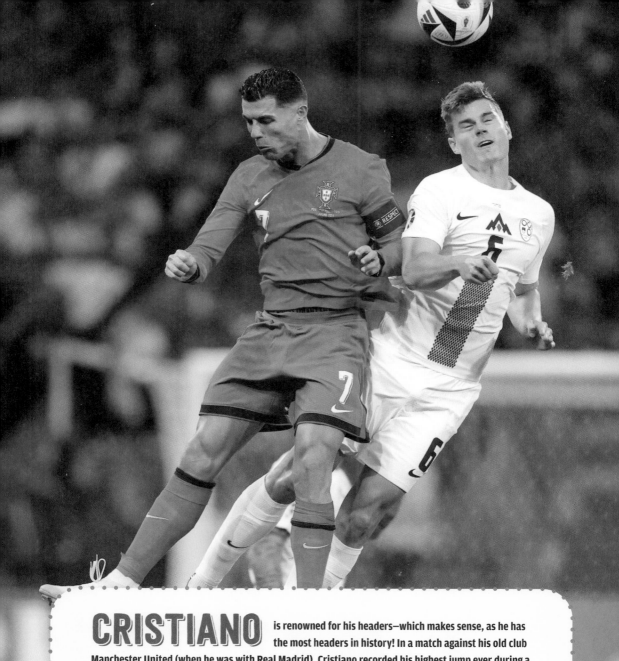

CRISTIANO is renowned for his headers—which makes sense, as he has the most headers in history! In a match against his old club Manchester United (when he was with Real Madrid), Cristiano recorded his highest jump ever during a header, flying high at 9 feet, 7 inches (2.9 m). That's the equivalent of 13 soccer balls stacked top of each other. His vertical leap at the time was 41.7 inches (1.1 m). To compare, the typical NBA vertical is 28 inches (71 cm) and Michael Jordan had a 48-inch (1.2 m) vertical leap.

For the first time, Cristiano was the elder statesman of the team. He had seen everything and was happy to mentor players and share his wisdom. Cristiano's teammate Giorgio Chiellini was overcome, witnessing firsthand his endless drive for perfection. Giorgio once said of Cristiano, "I was so fortunate to play with him. Seeing a player of that caliber with so much humbleness and respect for everyone was something beautiful. He never missed a team dinner."

In his three years with Juventus, Cristiano scored 101 goals in 134 appearances across all competitions. That's 0.75 goals per game and a goal every 114 minutes. In the Serie A league, he scored 81 goals in 98 matches and, after only 131 games, became the fastest player in Juventus history to reach 100 goals. He also became the first player to score 100 goals in three major leagues (Premier League, La Liga, Serie A). In the 2019–20 season, Cristiano scored 37 goals, the most a player has ever scored in a single season for Juventus. While wearing the black-and-white stripes of Juventus, he helped his team win five trophies: two Serie A titles, one Coppa Italia, and two Supercoppa Italiana.

BACK AND FORTH

After his three years with Juventus, Cristiano felt something calling him. The football world was stunned when he made the unexpected announcement that, after 12 years away, he would return to Manchester United. On September 11, 2021, Cristiano walked onto the pitch in that familiar red jersey. In true CR7 flair, he marked his grand return with two goals in a 4–1 victory over Newcastle United. His return also helped him reach yet another milestone. In 2022, Cristiano had a hat trick (only his second in the Premier League) against Tottenham Hotspur and surpassed Josef Bican's record of 805 career goals, becoming the all-time top scorer in competitive matches.

TOTTENHAM HOTSPUR

play in the only stadium specifically designed for NFL games outside North America. It's the third largest stadium in the UK and has the world's first dividing, retractable football pitch, which reveals a synthetic turf field underneath for NFL games. According to NFL research, the UK has nearly 14.3 million NFL fans—that's almost 1 in 5 people in the country.

Unfortunately, Cristiano's reunion tour wasn't all smooth sailing. Manchester United, despite having a burst of energy with Cristiano's return, struggled to be consistent. Cristiano scored 24 goals in 38 appearances in the 2021–22 season, including 18 Premier League goals, the third most in the league. Then, in 2021, the Man United manager, Ole Gunnar Solskjaer, was replaced with Erik ten Hag. The new manager clashed with Cristiano and had him sitting on the bench for much of the 2022–23 season. The team ultimately finished in sixth place that season. With tension running high between coach and player, Cristiano scored just 3 goals in sixteen appearances.

In December 2022, Cristiano signed a contract with the Saudi Arabian club Al-Nassr that was reportedly worth over $200 million per year. This made him the highest-paid footballer in history. Many famous soccer players choose to end their careers by going to less competitive leagues or simply retiring. Once more, Cristiano was carving his own path.

THE SAUDI PRO LEAGUE was founded in 1976 and is the top professional soccer league in Saudi Arabia. Consisting of 16 teams and with a season that runs from August to May, the most successful club in league history is Al-Hilal with 18 titles.

In his first press conference after moving to the Saudi Pro League, Cristiano said, "I'm a unique player. It's good to come here. I broke all the records [in Europe] and I want to break a few records here." As always, Cristiano's play elevated the league's popularity. His first season, he scored 14 goals in 16 league appearances. The team finished in second place, narrowly missing out on a title.

This time, the hardest part of adapting to a new league, team, and country was the intense heat of Saudi Arabia, which often exceeded 104°F (40°C). Cristiano carried out his training schedules later in the day when it was cooler and made sure to stay hydrated. As of September 2024, Cristiano has 68 goals in 74 appearances.

Cristiano joined Portugal once more for the 2024 Euros. At age 39, he became the first player to feature in six European Championships. During the group stage, Cristiano reminded the world of his skill by scoring his 900th career goal. Despite this incredible achievement, Cristiano went scoreless in all five games at Euro 2024 and Portugal was eliminated by France, a foe they had beaten eight years earlier.

CRISTIANO

is the all-time leading goal scorer in the European Championship, with 14 goals across five tournaments: 2004, 2008, 2012, 2016, and 2020. He is also the only player ever to have scored in five different European Championships.

ALL-TIME GOAL SCORER

From dusty streets to packed stadiums, Cristiano, the boy from Madeira, named after an American president, has repeatedly defied expectations, shattered unbreakable records, and stamped his name into the very fabric of soccer. His story reflects the transformative power of relentless determination and unwavering self-belief. He didn't just play the game; he redefined it. He is more than an athlete—he is a symbol of what can be achieved when talent meets tenacity.

Cristiano will forever be remembered as the skinny kid from a small island who dared to dream big—and, in the process, changed the game forever.

CHAPTER

OFF THE
PITCH

WORK BEYOND SOCCER

Beyond all the broken records, the remarkable goals, and the laundry list of accolades is a fascinating human being whose footprint in history is more than just what he does with a soccer ball. Over the years, Cristiano has built dozens of sprawling business empires, partnered with the biggest brands and sponsors, shown the world his philanthropic passions, and proudly helped shape the lives of his children and family. These endeavors showcase his relentless drive to leave a lasting legacy beyond his football career.

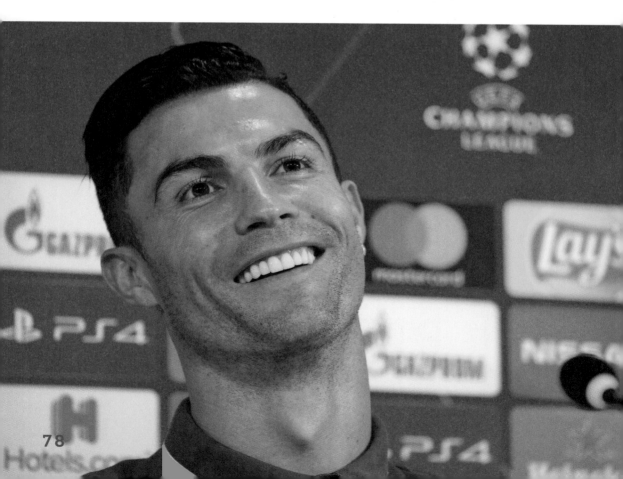

The Soccer Ball

- The earliest soccer balls were made from animal bladders (often pig or sheep) inflated with air and wrapped in leather.

- Charles Goodyear created the first mass-produced soccer ball in 1855. He used vulcanized rubber to make the ball more durable. (This is the same Goodyear that makes **tires** and has the famous blimp!)

- The **classic black-and-white soccer ball** (with 32 panels— 20 hexagons and 12 pentagons) was first used in the 1970 World Cup, designed to be easily visible on black-and-white television.

- The fastest recorded soccer ball kick was by Brazilian soccer player Ronny Heberson in 2006, coming in at 132 miles per hour (212 km/h).

132 mph!

- If you ask memorabilia experts, the most famous soccer ball was the one used for **Diego Maradona**'s "Hand of God" goal in the 1986 World Cup, which he punched past England's goalkeeper for a controversial goal. It sold in 2022 for $2.4 million.

When it comes to Cristiano's brands, CR7 stands above the rest. It has become a global phenomenon, encompassing everything from hotels and clothing lines to fragrances, footwear, and more. One of the main projects is a partnership with Pestana Hotel Group, which started the CR7 hotel brand with locations in Madeira, Lisbon, Madrid, New York, and Marrakech (with Paris to be added in 2027). These hotels reflect Cristiano's standard of excellence and offer a high-class experience the superstar has come to expect. Some hotels even allow you to reserve a room with an autographed soccer ball and postcard waiting when you check in!

Cristiano's largest and most significant endorsement deal is a lifetime contract with Nike. He is one of only four athletes with a lifetime contract, along with basketball players Michael Jordan (the first), LeBron James, and Kevin Durant (most recently).

AN IMPORTANT
LEGACY

While Cristiano's business ventures are very impressive, giving back is what's most important to him. He often uses his massive wealth and influence to make generous donations to hospitals, charities, and disaster relief efforts. In 2014, he was asked to donate a signed shirt and cleats to Erik Ortiz Cruz, a 10-month-old boy who suffered from cortical dysplasia (a condition causing up to 30 seizures a day), so the family could auction them off to pay for a special surgery. He sent the signed items along with $83,000 to pay for the entire surgery. He has also paid for cancer treatment for children, donated over $165,000 to the cancer center that treated his mother, donated to childhood cancer centers money won in court cases against British tabloids, fundraised for children fighting leukemia, and in 2017, raised $644,652 for the Make-A-Wish Foundation by auctioning off a replica of his second Ballon d'Or.

THE
MAKE-A-WISH
FOUNDATION

grants life-changing wishes to children with critical illnesses and gives them experiences that bring hope and joy during challenging times. From meeting a hero to going on a dream vacation, Make-A-Wish creates unforgettable memories for children and their families. To learn more or donate to help wishes come true, visit www.wish.org.

Cristiano has proven that he will show up to help during times of great distress or disaster. During the COVID-19 pandemic in 2020, Cristiano and his agent, **Jorge Mendes**, donated over $1 million to hospitals in Portugal for ventilators and medical equipment. During the Turkey-Syria earthquake in 2023, Cristiano contributed over $350,000 to recovery efforts that helped provide food, tents, blankets, beds, baby food, and medical supplies. One of the most heartwarming stories of all was in response to the Indonesia tsunami and earthquakes of 2004. Cristiano was moved by the heart-wrenching story of a seven-year-old named Martunis, who survived the deadly tsunami but was stranded wearing a Portugal jersey on a beach for 21 days. Cristiano flew out to meet the boy, befriended him, and eventually paid for his education. They formed a lasting bond—years later, with Martunis back on his feet, he joined the same Sporting CP youth program where Cristiano began his own career.

In addition to being a global ambassador for organizations like Save the Children, **UNICEF**, and World Vision, and helping fund initiatives that provide food, education, and healthcare to those in need, Cristiano is a regular blood donor. It's his way of proving that small actions can make a big difference in someone's life.

In his hometown of Madeira, he has contributed to many community projects and local hospitals. The CR7 Museum in Madeira, run by Cristiano's brother Hugo, is a huge tourist attraction highlighting his achievements and memorabilia. Madeira even named its airport Cristiano Ronaldo International Airport, proudly displaying its most famous resident and welcoming guests from around the world.

Cristiano's values stem from his upbringing. Despite immense fame and fortune, he's remained grounded thanks to his family. Since 2016, he's been with his partner, **Georgina Rodríguez**, a model and influencer, who Cristiano first met while she was working at a luxury store in Madrid. Like Cristiano, she's a public figure, now known for her Netflix series, *I Am Georgina*, on which she shares a unique view of her life and partnership with Cristiano. Georgina (or Gia as Cristiano calls her) appears regularly on Cristiano's YouTube channel, giving fans a glimpse of their close bond and the loving family they've created. Cristiano is very protective of his family and is famously very private, seldom giving out details to the media. Much of his desire for privacy started with the birth of his first son, **Cristiano Jr**.

Surprisingly Famous
JUNIORS

Many of the world's most famous faces are actually Juniors (or named after their father—just like Cristiano, Jr.). Still, we never call them by that name. Do you know these Juniors?

- **Snoop Dogg** (rapper): born Calvin Cordozar Broadus Jr.

- **Floyd Mayweather** (boxer): born Floyd Mayweather Jr.

- **Kurt Vonnegut** (author): born Kurt Vonnegut Jr.

- **Will Smith** (actor/rapper): born Willard Carroll Smith Jr.

- **Lil Wayne** (rapper): born Dwayne Michael Carter Jr.

FAMILY TIES

Cristiano's path to fatherhood began in 2010 when Cristiano Jr. was born. In 2017, Cristiano Jr. was joined by twin siblings, Eva and Mateo. Quickly after, Ronaldo's family grew with the arrival of a daughter, Alana Martina, with his partner, Georgina. Then, in 2022, Cristiano and Georgina dealt with a terrible tragedy; Georgina gave birth to a set of twins, a girl, Bella Esmerelda, and a boy, Angel. Angel did not survive. Still, the family keeps his memory alive every day.

Each of Cristiano's kids is a source of love and inspiration that fuels him to be the best on the field to provide for his family. Cristiano's family represents a softer side to the soccer star. He sees them as being just as important as any goal he's scored.

645 million followers

With over 645 million followers on Instagram, Cristiano is the most followed person in the world. Fans connect with him worldwide and gain glimpses into his life as an athlete and philanthropist. He inspires millions of young people to dream big, work hard, and give back. While on paper his legacy may be goals, wins, or trophies, his true impact lies in how he uses his many successes to help others. Cristiano's life off the pitch embodies the idea that greatness, however you want to define it, is not just about what someone can achieve but how they use their power to make the world a better place.

CHAPTER

STOPPAGE
TIME

CRISTIANO RONALDO
TOP FIVES

B elow are lists of some of the best Cristiano moments from his various accomplishments on the pitch. Check them out to learn from the best!

FREE KICKS

1. 2008–09 Champions League, Manchester United vs. Arsenal (40-yard screamer)
2. 2009, Manchester United vs. Portsmouth (signature Ronaldo knuckleball)
3. 2003, Manchester United vs. Portsmouth (first free kick goal/first goal for Man Utd)
4. 2007, Manchester United vs. Sporting CP (scores against former club where he never scored a free kick before)
5. 2022, Manchester United vs. Norwich (free kick goal equals hat trick for Cristiano)

HEADERS

1. **2012–13 Champions League, Real Madrid vs. Manchester United**
2. **Serie A 2019–20, Juventus vs. Sampdoria**
3. **Euro 2016, Portugal vs. Wales**
4. **2007–08 Champions League, Manchester United vs. Roma**
5. **2009, Manchester United vs. Tottenham**

CRISTIANO RONALDO

has the most goals in history with over 900 (and counting)! Against the same opponent, he has scored the most (27) versus Sevilla FC. Of those record-breaking 900 goals, he's scored 585 with his right foot, 177 with his left foot, and 152 with his head. Two of his goals came off his thigh and elbow! Cristiano's aim is to get 1,000 goals in his lifetime.

GOALS

1. 2017–18 Champions League, Real Madrid vs. Juventus (overhead bicycle kick)
2. 2008–09 Champions League, Manchester United vs. Porto*
3. 2024 Nations League, Portugal vs. Croatia (his 900th goal)
4. 2016, Real Madrid vs Espanyol
5. 2002, Sporting CP vs Moreirense (his first goal)

*This goal, made from 40 yards away, was clocked at 64.2 miles per hour (103.3 km/h) and earned Ronaldo the very first FIFA Puskás Award, honoring the most beautiful goal of the year.

HAT TRICKS

A "hat trick" is a term used in soccer and hockey for when a player scores three goals in one game.

1. 2019, Juventus vs. Atletico Madrid
2. 2018 World Cup, Portugal vs. Spain
3. 2014 World Cup, Portugal vs. Sweden
4. 2015–16 Champions League, Real Madrid vs. Wolfsburg
5. 2016–17 Champions League, Real Madrid vs. Bayern Munich

BEST KITS

1. 2008–09, Manchester United Home
2. 2014–15, Real Madrid Home
3. 2019–20, Juventus Home
4. 2004, Portugal Home
5. 2002–03, Sporting CP Home

EPIC RIVALRIES IN SPORTS

Epic rivalries have existed throughout history, but the greatest ones always seem to occur in the wide world of sports. Inspired by the epic battles and rivalry between Ronaldo and Messi (although *they* say there isn't a rivalry), here's a list of the most famous rivalries in sports!

BOSTON RED SOX VS. NEW YORK YANKEES

This rivalry, which started in 1901, is one of the most famous in *any* sport. The fans of each city take it seriously. It even resulted in a curse! After over 2,200 meetings, the Yankees are currently on top in the all-time standings.

USA 33

BABE RUTH

The Curse of the Bambino

In 1920, the Boston Red Sox sold legendary player Babe Ruth (nicknamed "The Bambino") to the New York Yankees. At the time, the Red Sox had won 5 World Series titles in 15 years and were the best team in baseball. After selling Ruth, they entered a period of decline. In contrast, the Yankees, with their new star, became the most successful team in baseball history, winning 4 championships with Ruth and 26 total up to the present time. Fans called it "The Curse of the Bambino," suggesting that selling Ruth doomed the Red Sox. The weight of "the curse" grew with each heartbreaking loss for decades. It was finally broken in 2004, when the Red Sox won the World Series and ended the longest drought in MLB history.

LARRY BIRD VS. MAGIC JOHNSON

The rivalry between these two legends began when they faced off in the 1979 NCAA championship and continued into the NBA throughout the 1980s. **Bird**'s Celtics and **Magic**'s Lakers met in three NBA Finals, with Magic winning two out of three. This rivalry turned basketball into a marquee sport, elevating the NBA by transforming it into a mainstream spectacle.

CHICAGO BEARS VS. GREEN BAY PACKERS

The oldest rivalry in NFL history started in 1921 with over 200 matchups. The series is close, but thanks in large part to quarterbacks Brett Favre and Aaron Rodgers, the Packers currently have the edge in wins between these iconic Midwestern franchises.

THE ROCK VS. STONE COLD STEVE AUSTIN

Iconic trash talk. Intense stare-downs. WrestleMania matches. The rivalry between Dwayne "The Rock" Johnson and Stone Cold Steve Austin is one of the most memorable in wrestling history.

DIRECT FROM RINGSIDE · EVERY THRILLING MOMENT
POPULAR PRICES
FIGHT PICTURES
ROUND BY ROUND · BLOW BY BLOW
BATTLE OF THE CHAMPIONS
IN COLOR
JOE FRAZIER
VS.
MUHAMMAD ALI

CASSIUS CLAY

JOE FRAZIER

WILL NOT BE SHOWN ON HOME TV FOR 6 MONTHS!

MUHAMMAD ALI VS. JOE FRAZIER

Despite only facing each other in the ring three times, these two boxing heavyweights have one of the greatest rivalries in boxing. Their first fight in 1971 was dubbed the "Fight of the Century" and their last in 1975 was the famous "Thrilla in Manila." Ali won two out of three bouts.

ROGER FEDERER VS. RAFAEL NADAL VS. NOVAK DJOKOVIC

Known as the "Big Three" in professional tennis, this trio has dominated men's tennis for two decades, winning a collective 66 Grand Slam titles. **Djokovic** leads with 24, followed by Nadal with 22 (and a record 14 French Opens) and Federer with 20. With 150 head-to-head matches and numerous world number-one rankings, their dominance defined a golden era of tennis.

IN TENNIS,

a "Grand Slam" refers to the four most prestigious tournaments in the sport: the Australian Open, the French Open, Wimbledon, and the US Open. If a player wins all four in the same calendar year, they achieve a Calendar Grand Slam.

COLLINGWOOD F.C. VS. CARLTON F.C.

In addition to the sport known around the world as football and American football, there's also Australian football. This fast-paced, exciting game (combining aspects of soccer, volleyball, and basketball) has been around for nearly 150 years. The fiercest rivalry in the Australian Football League (AFL) is between the Collingwood Magpies and Carlton Blues, two clubs in Melbourne with loyal fans who make their fandom a way of life. The teams are in a three-way tie (with Essendon F.C.) with 16 championships each.

INSIDE THE WORLD OF
CRISTIANO RONALDO

You've watched him score jaw-dropping goals, outrun and outsmart the world's best defenders, and lead his teams to championship glory on the biggest stages. But how well do you know Cristiano Ronaldo off the pitch? Dive into some awesome and surprising facts about the global superstar!

Astrological Sign

Aquarius

Favorite Movie

Cristiano usually prefers documentaries so he can learn new facts.

Childhood Idols

Brazilian soccer stars Ronaldo Nazario and Ronaldinho.

If he could play with one player in soccer history, it would be . . .

Eusebio, one of Portugal's greatest soccer players, nicknamed "The Black Panther."

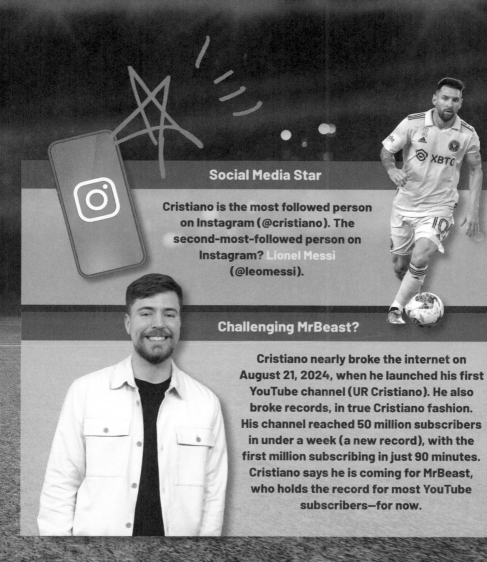

Social Media Star

Cristiano is the most followed person on Instagram (@cristiano). The second-most-followed person on Instagram? Lionel Messi (@leomessi).

Challenging MrBeast?

Cristiano nearly broke the internet on August 21, 2024, when he launched his first YouTube channel (UR Cristiano). He also broke records, in true Cristiano fashion. His channel reached 50 million subscribers in under a week (a new record), with the first million subscribing in just 90 minutes. Cristiano says he is coming for MrBeast, who holds the record for most YouTube subscribers—for now.

Favorite Music

Cristiano loves to listen to all types of music. He often finds a song he loves and plays it repeatedly (according to Gia). Some of his favorite artists are Sade, Phil Collins, Elton John, George Michael, and Brazilian artist Ivete Sangalo.

Favorite Sport (Other Than Soccer)

Though he likes to watch combat sports like boxing or MMA, Cristiano loves Ping-Pong!

DURING AN INTERVIEW,

Cristiano's former Manchester United teammate Patrice Evra described when Cristiano lost a Ping-Pong match against teammate Rio Ferdinand that they played in front of the whole team. Furious at the loss, Cristiano asked his cousin to buy him a Ping-Pong table. After training for two weeks, he came back and beat Rio. Talk about competitive spirit!

Universal Appeal

In 2015, astronomers discovered one of the brightest and oldest galaxies 12.9 billion light-years away. They named it Cosmos Redshift 7 (CR7) in honor of Cristiano Ronaldo.

Favorite Color

White. Cristiano loves white sneakers and thinks he looks best wearing white.

IF NASA

said you could name a new star or galaxy, what would you call it and why?

To Ink or Not to Ink

Unlike many professional athletes of this generation, Cristiano has no tattoos. Why? So he can donate blood more often without a waiting period. He actively promotes blood donation and is also a registered bone marrow donor.

Speed Demon

In 2024, at age 39, Cristiano was clocked during a Euros game running 20.3 miles per hour (32.7 km/h)!

Favorite Food

Bacalhau à Brás, a traditional Portuguese dish made with shredded salted cod, onions, finely diced fried potatoes, and scrambled eggs.

The Right Foot Forward

Cristiano always steps onto the pitch with his right foot forward. Many think it's a superstition (which it may be at this point), but there's a saying in Portuguese culture: *entra com a direita*. This means "enter with the right," so it's also a way to respect his culture.

Car Enthusiast

Cristiano has one of the most expensive car collections in the world, worth over $25 million. He owns a $9 million Bugatti Centodieci and cars from other high-end brands such as Ferrari, McLaren, Lamborghini, Rolls-Royce, Bentley, and Porsche.

THE GOLDEN FOOT

As the saying goes, "Records are meant to be broken." In the world of soccer, Cristiano Ronaldo is a wrecking ball. He's broken so many records that he'll probably have even more records on his resume by the time you read this. This list features just the highlights of his illustrious career, including individual achievements, team accolades, records broken, and a handful of personal accomplishments deserving of one of the most decorated athletes in history!

Long-Running CAREERS

Professional sports can take their toll on an athlete's body. The average athlete only lasts a limited number of years in their respective sport: NFL (3.3 years), NBA (4.5 years), NHL (5 years), MLB (5.6 years), soccer (8 to 11 years), tennis (14 to 18 years). However, Cristiano has lasted 22 years so far! In honor of his longevity, here are some of the longest-tenured athletes in sports history.

Gordie Howe (Hockey)
Career length: 32 years (1946-80)
Retirement age: 52
Teams: Detroit Red Wings, Houston Aeros, New England Whalers, Hartford Whalers

Tom Brady (Football)
Career length: 23 years (2000-23)
Retirement age: 45
Teams: New England Patriots, Tampa Bay Buccaneers

Martina Navratilova (Tennis)
Career Length: 31 years (1975-2006)
Retirement age: 50

Vince Carter (Basketball)
Career length: 22 years* (1998-2020)
Retirement age: 43
Teams: Toronto Raptors, New Jersey Nets, Orlando Magic, Phoenix Suns, Dallas Mavericks, Memphis Grizzlies, Sacramento Kings, Atlanta Hawks
*Tied with LeBron James.

Satchel Paige (Baseball)
Career length: 40 years (1926-66)
Retirement age: 59 years
Teams: (Negro Leagues) Chattanooga Black Lookouts, Birmingham Black Barons, Cleveland Cubs, Pittsburgh Crawfords, Kansas City Monarchs, New York Black Yankees; (MLB) Cleveland Guardians, St. Louis Browns

INDIVIDUAL
ACCOLADES

(as of the end of the 2023–2024 season)

- **7x Champions League Top Scorer** (2008, 2013, 2014, 2015, 2016, 2017, 2018)
- **5x Ballon d'Or** (2008, 2013, 2014, 2016, 2017)
- **4x European Golden Shoe** (2008, 2011, 2014, 2015)
- **3x La Liga Pichichi Trophy** (2011, 2014, 2015)
- **3x UEFA Men's Player of the Year Award** (2013–14, 2014–15, 2015–16)
- **2x The Best FIFA Men's Player Award** (2016, 2017)
- **2x Serie A Footballer of the Year** (2019, 2020)
- **FIFA World Player of the Year** (2008)
- **FIFA Puskás Award** (2009)
- **FIFA Club World Cup Golden Ball** (2016)

- **Premier League Golden Boot** (2008)*
- **Serie A Capocannoniere Award** (2021)
- **Saudi Pro League Golden Boot** (2024)
- **UEFA European Championship Golden Boot** (2020)
- **La Liga Best Player** (2013–14)

* * * * * * * * * * * *

*One of only five players (along with Thierry Henry, Kevin Phillips, Luis Suárez, Erling Haaland) to win the Premier League Golden Boot and European Golden Shoe in the same year.

RECORDS HELD OR BROKEN

- Most international caps/appearances (217)
- Most goals all-time (900 and counting)
- Most international goals in football history (131, Portugal)
- All-time top scorer for Portugal (135)
- First male player to score in five World Cups
- Most goals in a single season for Juventus (37)
- Most goals in a single season for Manchester United (31)
- All-time top scorer for Real Madrid (450)
- Most goals scored in a single Saudi Pro League season (35)
- All-time top scorer in the Champions League (140)
- First player to score 100 goals for three different clubs (Manchester United, Real Madrid, Juventus)

- Most hat tricks scored in the Champions League (8)
- Most international hat tricks (10)*
- Most header goals (152)
- Only player in history to three-peat the Premier League and the Champions League
- First player to score in every minute of a football game (1–90)
- First player to appear in six European Championships

• • • • • • • • • • • • • •

*Tied with Lionel Messi.

- Most goals in a single Champions League season (17)

ACCOLADES

- 4x FIFA Club World Cups (2008, 2015, 2017, 2018)
- 4x Champions League Titles with Real Madrid (2014, 2016, 2017, 2018)
- 3x Premier League Titles with Manchester United (2007, 2008, 2009)
- 2x La Liga Titles with Real Madrid (2012, 2017)
- 2x Serie A Titles with Juventus (2019, 2020)
- 2x UEFA Super Cups with Real Madrid (2014, 2017)
- 2x Copas del Rey with Real Madrid (2011, 2014)

- 2x Spanish Super Cups with Real Madrid (2012, 2017)
- 2x EFL Cup Champions with Manchester United (2006, 2009)
- 2x Supercoppa Italiana with Juventus (2018, 2020)
- UEFA Nations League with Portugal (2019)
- Coppa Italia with Juventus (2021)
- FA Cup Champion with Manchester United (2004)
- Champions League title with Manchester United (2008)
- European Championship title with Portugal (2016)

PERSONAL

ACCOMPLISHMENTS

- 4x ESPY Award Winner for Best International Athlete (2014, 2016, 2018, 2021)
- 4x *Forbes* World's Highest-Paid Athlete (2016, 2017, 2023, 2024)
- Most Charitable Sportsperson by DoSomething.org (2015)

- *Time* 100 Most Influential People (2014)
- Grand Officer of the Order of Prince Henry (2014), one of Portugal's highest honors
- Global Ambassador

THE ULTIMATE
CRISTIANO RONALDO
QUIZ

—

Having read this far, you should be an expert on Cristiano Ronaldo. Why don't we put it to the test? Below are 10 questions about Cristiano's life and career. Quiz yourself or your friends and family, and after you're done, let's see if you shout "Siiuuuuuu" like Cristiano!

1 What famous figure did Cristiano's parents name him after because they were great admirers of this person's work?

    A. Ronaldinho Gaúcho

    B. Christian Dior

    C. Ronald Reagan

    D. Christopher Reeve

 **IF YOU COULD** trade any part of your name (first, middle, last) with any name in the world, what would it be and why?

2 In the deal that sent Cristiano to C.D. Nacional (his second club), what did C.F. Andorinha get in return?

    A. $500

    B. A new set of goals

    C. $2,500

    D. 20 soccer balls and 2 sets of kits

3 Cristiano has played (and dominated) in all but which of the following professional soccer leagues?

    A. Bundesliga

    B. Serie A

    C. English Premier League

    D. La Liga

4 While playing for Sporting CP in Lisbon, what medical condition sidelined 15-year-old Cristiano and required fast action by doctors?

    A. Asthma

    B. Tachycardia

    C. Migraines

    D. Bradycardia

5 In 2004, Cristiano had the honor of playing for his home country of Portugal in his first-ever Euros. In the final match, what country pulled an upset and defeated Portugal to win it all?

    A. Spain

    B. Germany

    C. France

    D. Greece

6 Everyone knows about the famous rivalry between Cristiano Ronaldo and Lionel Messi. But do you remember the name given to any match between Lionel Messi's FC Barcelona and Cristiano's Real Madrid?

A. El Derbi Madrileño   C. El Clásico

B. La Epica Juego   D. La Gran Batalla

 7 What is the name of the coach (a soccer legend) who insisted Cristiano wear the number 7 jersey because of how special he was on the field?

A. Sir Matt Busby   C. Sir Walter Winterbottom

B. Sir Alex Ferguson   D. Sir Bobby Rosen

The Name of the GAME

Several famous sporting matchups have catchy names to honor an intense rivalry. Here are a few to impress your friends with the next time they happen!

- **"The Ashes":** England vs. Australia (cricket)
- **"The Iron Bowl":** Auburn vs. Alabama (college football)
- **"The Crosstown Classic":** Chicago Cubs vs. Chicago White Sox (baseball)
- **"The Battle of Alberta":** Calgary Flames vs. Edmonton Oilers (hockey)
- **"The Merseyside Derby":** Liverpool vs. Everton (soccer)

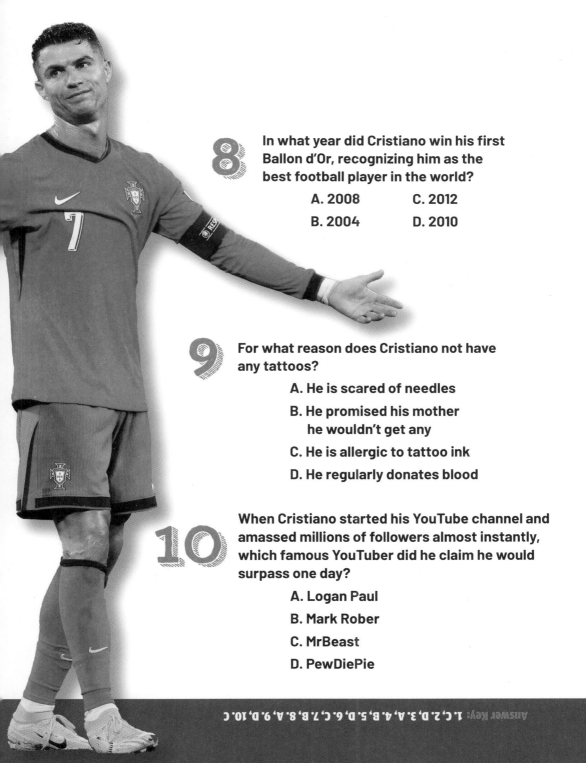

8 In what year did Cristiano win his first Ballon d'Or, recognizing him as the best football player in the world?

A. 2008   C. 2012

B. 2004   D. 2010

9 For what reason does Cristiano not have any tattoos?

A. He is scared of needles

B. He promised his mother he wouldn't get any

C. He is allergic to tattoo ink

D. He regularly donates blood

10 When Cristiano started his YouTube channel and amassed millions of followers almost instantly, which famous YouTuber did he claim he would surpass one day?

A. Logan Paul

B. Mark Rober

C. MrBeast

D. PewDiePie

CHAPTER

CR7 AT HOME

A DAY IN THE LIFE OF
CRISTIANO RONALDO

t's no secret that Cristiano is considered one of the most fit humans on Earth. He maintains such an incredible physique through hard work and discipline. We've gathered some of Cristiano's methods and incorporated them into easy-to-remember categories so you can bring the CR7 lifestyle into your own daily routine!

EAT

Instead of three big meals, Cristiano eats five or six small meals a day every two to four hours to aid in metabolism and have a steady stream of healthy energy. His meals are packed with lean proteins (fish, chicken, eggs) and heavy in vegetables, whole grains, and fruits. He avoids sugary foods and drinks, keeping hydrated with water.

DURING A EURO 2020

press conference, Cristiano moved two Coca-Cola bottles away from him. He held up a water bottle, saying, "Water!" This gesture caused Coca-Cola's market value to drop $4 billion, underscoring Cristiano's impact as a global icon.

CR7 AT HOME

- Snack on fruits, yogurt, or nuts to keep energy up.
- Include lean protein and vegetables in your meals to stay strong.
- Replace sugary drinks with water—and always stay hydrated!

EXERCISE

Cristiano trains three to four hours a day, five days a week. His workouts include ice baths in the morning, cardio, weight training, soccer drills, and swimming to end the day. You don't have to copy his routine, but remember, fitness is important!

- Start your day with cardio, like a brisk 10-minute walk or bike ride.
- To stay disciplined in your routine, add calisthenics after waking or before bed.*
- Grab a friend or partner to help push each other and stay accountable.

*Calisthenics are exercises that use your body weight and don't require equipment. All you need is yourself! Examples include sit-ups, squats, and push-ups.

SLEEP

Unlike most of us who try to sleep for eight hours every night, Cristiano doesn't sleep all in one go. He likes to take several 90-minute naps, or bursts of sleep, throughout the day to give his muscles time to recover. Cristiano believes proper rest is just as important as training so you can perform at your best!

- Try to get at least 8 hours of sleep each night to help you recover and grow.
- After strenuous activity, take a 20-minute power nap.
- To aid your sleep, turn off all screens and other distractions.

RELAX

Cristiano unwinds by listening to music, spending quality time with his family, and practicing mindfulness (or meditation) to keep himself centered. A healthy mind means a healthy life.

CR7 AT HOME

- Listen to upbeat music for motivation and slower music or audiobooks to relax.
- Try to spend 5 minutes a day focusing on your breathing to clear your head.
- Take breaks to spend time with family or friends.

Do You Ever Feel Overwhelmed?

Sometimes, with all the activities we have in our day (school, chores, sports, homework), our mind can feel like it's having its own soccer match! What do you do to unwind or relax? Here are some mindfulness tips you can try.

- **Sit or lie down comfortably.** Close your eyes. Put your hands on your stomach.
- **Take big breaths** in (feel your stomach inflate) and long breaths out (feel it deflate).
- **Concentrate on your breaths** (and nothing else) for 5 minutes and open your eyes.

FOCUS

Goals are important to Cristiano, whether learning a new dribble, mastering a new skill, or surpassing fitness goals. Your own goals may be small, medium, or large, but the important thing is that you have something to work toward.

CR7 AT HOME

- Make your bed each morning and you'll have accomplished something before breakfast.
- Set small goals and check them off a list to show how much progress you've made.
- Always be learning. Read books, watch videos, and experience art in any form.

FINAL WORDS

If there's one thing Cristiano loves more than soccer, it's giving back to the world. But you don't have to be famous to make a difference. Try donating clothes, food, or toys to a local shelter or organizing a friendly game of soccer and making sure everyone takes part.

DONATION

EVERY WORLD CUP CHAMPION IN
FIFA HISTORY
(1930–2024)

2022 | Argentina	**1978** | Argentina
2018 | France	**1974** | West Germany
2014 | Germany	**1970** | Brazil
2010 | Spain	**1966** | England
2006 | Italy	**1962** | Brazil
2002 | Brazil	**1958** | Brazil
1998 | France	**1954** | West Germany
1994 | Brazil	**1950** | Uruguay
1990 | West Germany	**1938** | Italy
1986 | Argentina	**1934** | Italy
1982 | Italy	**1930** | Uruguay

EVERY OLYMPIC SOCCER
GOLD MEDALIST

—

MEN'S TOURNAMENT
(1900-PRESENT)

2024 | Spain	**1984** | France
2020 | Brazil	**1980** | Czechoslovakia
2016 | Brazil	**1976** | East Germany
2012 | Mexico	**1972** | Poland
2008 | Argentina	**1968** | Hungary
2004 | Argentina	**1964** | Hungary
2000 | Cameroon	**1960** | Yugoslavia
1996 | Nigeria	**1956** | Soviet Union
1992 | Spain	**1952** | Hungary
1988 | Soviet Union	**1948** | Sweden

1936 | Italy	**1912** | Great Britain
1928 | Uruguay	**1908** | Great Britain
1924 | Uruguay	**1904** | Canada
1920 | Belgium	**1900** | Great Britain

WOMEN'S TOURNAMENT (1996–PRESENT)

2024 | United States	**2012** | United States
2020 | Canada	**2008** | United States
2016 | Germany	**2004** | United States
	2000 | Norway
	1996 | United States

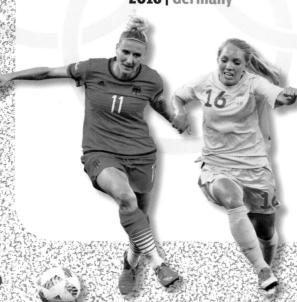

PHOTO CREDITS

ACKNOWLEDGMENTS

Cristiano was clearly born with talent, but to truly become great, he needed coaches and mentors. My first coach helped me throw a ball, swing a bat, and taught me the value of hard work. He's the best athlete I've ever known—and he happens to be my dad. This one's for you. Love you.

My life wouldn't be the same without the mentorship and guidance of my own creative triuMvirate – Diane Marelli, Kevin McOlgan, and Edward Mokrzycki—without whom I never would have dared to dream, let alone sing, drum, or act. Kids, listen to your teachers.

Thanks to my wife Colleen, my family, and my friends for their continued support. To my literary goalkeeper, Justin Brouckaert of Aevitas Creative Management, thanks for all the saves. To Katie McGuire and Cara Donaldson, you were phenomenal teammates. Nicole James, thanks for always passing me the ball. Quarto Kids, thanks for trusting me with this awesome series and for picking such an amazing design team. And to Cristiano Ronaldo—you're unfairly talented, ridiculously rich, and annoyingly handsome, but your heart is as big as your trophy cabinet. For that, I'll forgive you for setting unrealistic standards for what abs should look like.